A Note to Parents and Caregivers:

Read-it! Readers are for children who are just starting on the amazing road to reading. These beautiful books support both the acquisition of reading skills and the love of books.

 The PURPLE LEVEL presents basic topics and objects using high frequency words and simple language patterns.

 The RED LEVEL presents familiar topics using common words and repeating sentence patterns.

 The BLUE LEVEL presents new ideas using a larger vocabulary and varied sentence structure.

 The YELLOW LEVEL presents more challenging ideas, a broad vocabulary, and wide variety in sentence structure.

 The GREEN LEVEL presents more complex ideas, an extended vocabulary range, and expanded language structures.

 The ORANGE LEVEL presents a wide range of ideas and concepts using challenging vocabulary and complex language structures.

When sharing a book with your child, read in short stretches, pausing often to talk about the pictures. Have your child turn the pages and point to the pictures and familiar words. And be sure to reread favorite stories or parts of stories.

There is no right or wrong way to share books with children. Find time to read with your child, and pass on the legacy of literacy.

Adria F. Klein, Ph.D.
Professor Emeritus
California State University
San Bernardino, California

Editor: Christianne Jones
Designer: Lori Bye
Page Production: Michelle Biedscheid
Art Director: Nathan Gassman
The illustrations in this book were created with watercolor and pencil.

Picture Window Books
1710 Roe Crest Drive
North Mankato, MN 56003
www.capstonepub.com

Library of Congress Cataloging-in-Publication Data
Worsham, Adria F. (Adria Fay), 1947-
Max celebrates Groundhog Day / by Adria F. Worsham ; illustrated by Mernie
Gallagher-Cole.
p. cm. — (Read-it! readers. The life of Max)
ISBN 978-1-4048-4760-6 (library binding) ISBN 978-1-4048-8125-9 (paperback)
ISBN 978-1-4048-4764-4 (paperback)
[1. Groundhog Day—Fiction. 2. Woodchucks—Fiction. 3. School field trips—
Fiction.] I. Gallagher-Cole, Mernie, ill. II. Title.
PZ7.W887835Max 2008
[E]—dc22   2008006320

Printed in the United States of America in Stevens Point, Wisconsin.
072013   007509R

Max
Celebrates
Groundhog Day

by Adria F. Worsham
illustrated by Mernie Gallagher-Cole

Special thanks to our reading adviser:

Susan Kesselring, M.A., Literacy Educator
Rosemount–Apple Valley–Eagan (Minnesota) School District

PiCTURE WiNDOW BOOKS
Minneapolis, Minnesota

Max and Zoe are very excited.

They are going on a field trip with their classmates.

The teacher tells the class it is Groundhog Day.

They are going to the park to see the groundhog.

Lots of people are at the park.

There is going to be a special celebration for Groundhog Day.

The teacher tells the class about the groundhog.

The groundhog lives in a hole in the ground. It comes out to get food.

On Groundhog Day, the groundhog comes out of its hole and looks for its shadow.

Max and Zoe want to see
the groundhog.

They watch the hole in the ground.

On a sunny day, the groundhog will see its shadow. If the groundhog sees its shadow, it goes back into the hole.

The teacher says this means there will be six more weeks of winter.

Max shouts. He sees the groundhog come out of its hole.

Everyone is looking and pointing at the groundhog.

Today is a cloudy day. The groundhog cannot see its shadow.

The teacher says this means spring
will be here soon.

Max is glad that the groundhog did not see its shadow.

He is glad that spring will be here soon.